JUST BE MY FRIEND

by Hadley Read
and Mary Klaaren Andersen

January, 1987

Jim and Marlene:

Hadley would want you two to be one of the first recipient of this — his last manuscript, which, with co-author Mary Anderson was unfinished when he died. We decided to publish it ourselves in his memory.

In Friendship,

Margaret

The opening poem by Albert Camus is reprinted by permission of Random House, Inc., and Alfred A. Knopf, Inc.

The closing quotation is from the Revised Standard Version of the Bible.

Photo Credits:

Cover: Zehr Photography, Champaign, Illinois

Lyle Abbott, St. Louis, Missouri
Mary Andersen, Champaign, Illinois
Mary Beth, Urbana, Illinois
Bob Forsburg Photography, San Francisco, California
John Jamieson, Minneapolis, Minnesota
Eugene Klaaren, Middletown, Connecticut
Keith Klaaren, Holland, Michigan
Karyl Wackerlin, Champaign, Illinois

Published by: Mary Klaaren Andersen/The Read Family
             2002 Galen Drive
             Champaign, Illinois 61821

Printed by Crouse Printing & Mailing Service Co., Champaign, Illinois.

ISBN 0-9617924-0-X

Don't walk in front of me
I may not follow
Don't walk behind me
I may not lead
Walk beside me
and just be my friend.

Camus

For Friends

Preface

My co-author Hadley Read had a rare gift for friendship. Friends were not merely important to him; they were almost as necessary as food or air.

He made friends easily and kept them a long time. He cared about people, was an attentive listener, and loyal to a fault. His relationships were characterized by intensity, intimacy, and soul-baring communication.

The death of his youngest son at age 22 left a scar that never completely healed. As Phillip lay near death, his father, deeply moved, asked what he could do for him. Phillip replied, "Just be my friend." This later became a natural title for our book.

Hadley's circle of friends widened, partly because he was willing to risk talking with strangers wherever he happened to be. Sometimes, a follow-up call or note cemented the relationship. Some of the poems touch on the theme of chance encounters which turned into friendships.

Our friendship came about through a casual first meeting over coffee. We were both communicators by training, and both felt strongly about friendships, we discovered. This book was born at that time.

While a few poems were jointly authored, most were written individually. The poems were written as if spoken and are meant to be read aloud.

Hadley died while the manuscript was in rough form. Some months later, his wife Margaret, daughter Mary Read Beth and I decided to complete the work in Hadley's memory. We worked together to edit, refine, and publish the book. Son Gregory Read, in absentia, lent his support and encouragement.

Many others played a part in this venture. Shirley Crouse's patience and advice were invaluable. I am particularly grateful to my parents Marion and Cornelia Klaaren, husband Ken, son Erik, brother Keith, sister Joy Forgwe, and my brother and sister-in-law Eugene and Mary Klaaren. Also, the women of Third Reformed Church in Holland, Michigan, were an enthusiastic audience for my first reading of the poems and urged their publication. Then

there were friends who were sounding boards and those who kept asking how the book was coming.

Without friends, there would be no book, for the experiences of friendship are the seeds from which the poems grew. Perhaps you will recognize yourself in these pages.

Mary Klaaren Andersen
August, 1986
Champaign, Illinois

INTRODUCTION

In truth, it matters little that we define friendship.
It is one of life's great mysteries
and has meaning for each of us.

We move through our lives seeking that unique and elusive kind of relationship with others that will make us more complete human beings.

Rich or poor, famous or ordinary, we seek in others the missing parts of ourselves. We seek without always knowing why. We seek without always knowing how. Yet we know the search must go on, because we have come to understand that without friends we are so much less than we know we can be.

We thrill when a new friendship evolves, often unexpectedly. We grieve when an old friendship ends, often without understanding. We wonder how it is that we can be surrounded by people we know, with few we know as friends.

With a friend, the colors of our lives are brighter and in sharper focus. Without a friend, there is a persistent ache of loneliness. Mother Theresa touched on this theme when she said, in essence, that she found more hunger for love in America than hunger for food in all of India.

Often we seek the wisdom and words of others to understand the relationships we want and need. In a way, it is comforting to know that this search for the meaning of friendship is centuries old, perhaps as old as humanity itself. The familiar words of an Arab proverb beautifully express the nature of friendship. "A friend is one to whom one may pour out all of the contents of one's heart, chaff and grain together, knowing that the gentlest of hands will take and sift it, keep what is worth keeping and with a breath of kindness blow the rest away."

Friends often look outward in the same direction. They frequently share convictions of what matters most in life.

In contrast to so much else in our world, friendship is neither commercial nor programmed. It cannot be bought. Unlike business, therapeutic, or other contractual arrangements, friendship is entered into for its own sake. Yet its fruits are often surprising and profound. What can compare with the spontaneous opening of one heart to another? Sometimes friends can peel away the layers and be emotionally naked. Friends are society's natural healers because they *care.* Unlike jogging or yoga in heady, solitary search of self-fulfillment, friendship involves the nonselfconscious, natural sharing of life lived in relationship. By trusting and believing in each other and in each other's unique possibilities for growth during all the stages of life, friends literally pump new life into each other. Friends keep each other alive.

Yet on the dark side, friends can also let each other down, betray each other, and hurt each other as no one else can. When they speak from their innermost selves and confront each other with painful truths, they cut to the bone. Such encounters may weaken or destroy the friendship or strengthen and deepen it. There is always the potential for forgiveness and beginning anew.

In truth, we cannot capture friendship fully; it is one of life's great mysteries. Like life itself, it has a beginning, a time of growth and nurturing, and an ending, although there may be pain and sadness the ending has come about.

Through these pages we share our expressions of friendship and the art of being friends. We share without claiming special knowledge or wisdom but with the hope that our thoughts will encourage you to share with others. For when there is more sharing, there will be more friendship.

THE NATURE OF FRIENDSHIP

It seems to me
we do not really make friends —
we discover them.
Friendship is a Gift.

Friendship Is. . .

As confident as the touch of a child
holding your hand
As fragile as the wings of a butterfly
As elusive as a wisp of smoke
on a summer afternoon
As strong as a strand of steel
As comforting as a warming fire
on a cold winter day
And as joyous as life itself.

Seek less the definition of a friend
Seek more the art of being one.

Only Through His Friends

To some he is a witty man
who chases gloom away
with wry good-humored commentaries
*   on the logical absurdities of life.*

Others know him as a gentle heart
who listens to their hopes
then moves inside their very souls
to see them as they want to be.

Still others
seek the products of his thoughts
*   and marvel at the workings of his mind*
which seems to understand
*   the way things are.*

He is those things and more
but only through his friends
*   who make him whole.*

Father And Son

You ask
> *when you are young*
> *and the world in such chaos*
Is it not best
> *to avoid involvements*
> *to live life for yourself*
> *to be free from entanglements*
> *to go as many places as you can*
> *to see as many sights*
> *to do as many things.*

But is that possible
> *by yourself*
> > *without friends?*

So Long As You Have Need

Some friends are like misty rain
            on a warm spring morning
whispering softly so as not to disturb
                        refreshing
soothing with gentleness
promising when they leave
            to come again.

Some friends are like summer showers
bursting in on your life unexpectedly
                        laughing
shouting here I come ready or not
filling your cup with new excitement
                        promising nothing
but winking openly
to let you know they will return some day.

Some friends are like early fall rains
            that come in the night
comforting you with their presence
                        confident and steady
reassuring you with their strength
promising to be there
            so long as you have need.

Thank You

Do not thank me
if you deem me kind
    or thoughtful
        or generous.
Do not sing the praise of me
if I share my dreams with you
    my hopes
        and my fears.

It is I who should thank you
        dear friend
for inviting me into your life
to share such gifts with you
for letting me be
    who I want to be.

A Matter Of Time

They belonged to Junior League
> *and carpooled kids to nursery school*
> *and helped with the Girl Scout cookie sale*
> *and sometimes made a fourth for bridge*
but they didn't have time
> *to be friends.*

o o o

They both worked for the university
> *and served on the same committees*
> *and attended the meetings of the Quarterback Club*
> *and went to all the football games*
but they didn't have time
> *to be friends.*

o o o

They served on the Cancer Fund Drive
> *and headed committees for the Centennial Show*
> *and campaigned hard for the Mayor*
> *and served on the church welcoming board*
but they didn't have time
> *to be friends.*

Soul Mate

It wasn't so much that we both loved
               daisies
               wood floors
               writing letters
and thought of ourselves as peacemakers.

But when she told me
               she cried
when the call to do the supper dishes
broke the magic of one of those late-night-conversations
               around the kitchen table
I knew I'd found a soul mate.

More Than Companions

There were six of us

>*who enjoyed doing things together:*

>*taking walks, skating, going to movies,*
>*exercising, catching up on mending,*
>*shopping, having lunch,*
>>*or*
>*chatting lightly*
>>*about anything.*

Then two of us
>*chanced upon*
>>*More.*

We cared about the same things.
No wonder we asked the same questions
and thirsted for what the other gave
>>*though our answers often differed.*
We explored together
>>*our inner journeys.*
We were close friends.

Grandfather And Grandson

Four hands on the wheel
  two small chocolate ones
  two huge pale ones
Two happy faces
  tight black curls beneath the graying stubble
Speeding along together
  totem-style.

The grandson had just come from nursery school
  where he went to be socialized
    with kids his age.
But he wasn't turned on putt-putting on tricycles
  with kids whose noses ran
    like his.
The grandfather had just come from ministers' meeting
  where he went to stay active
    in his calling.
But he didn't like being classed
  with the retirees.
He wondered where their wonder went.

One big hand off the wheel
  jabbing and roaring
    "Look at that flock of geese."
Two heads out the window
    totem-style still
    "Grandpa, they're friends."
    "Why?"
    "They're flying together."

Strange World, Isn't It

Adam likes to hunt and fish.
Erik likes to read and listen to symphonies.

Adam likes to build things with his hands.
Erik likes to build things with his mind.

Adam belongs to Rotary and calls everyone Brother.
Erik belongs to Bird Watchers and goes out alone.

Adam plays poker and drinks beer.
Erik plays bridge and drinks dry wine.

Adam is in the construction business.
Erik is in the teaching business.

Why is it so strange
that each considers the other
            his best friend?

The Best Medicine

When you needed to find her
you listened for
        her laugh.

A few thought her too funny, almost flip.
They tried to figure out what made her tick
because when everyone else let it all hang out
        she didn't.

She wasn't her work
her children
her house
her hobbies
her husband.
        She just was.

She never gave advice
except once I asked and what she said
went straight to the heart of the matter
        — my heart —
we laughed and laughed and laughed.
(Psychotherapy could never do that.)
Don't be so vulnerable, she said.
You're too defenseless.
But when I touched on a certain subject
her soul spilled out —
        two tears escaped.

Is that why she laughs?

A Gift

I do not know
> *how we became friends*
> *when*
>> *or*
> *why.*
But I do know
> *we are.*

I did not set out to be his friend
> *did not do things with that in mind.*
I was just myself
> *letting fly half-hatched remarks*
> *that he said gave him perspective*
> *and made him laugh.*

It seems to me
we do not really make friends —
we discover them.
Friendship is a Gift.

More Than A Book

When I was losing my path
a friend led me
*   to a passage in a book*
*   that spoke to him.*

The book was the kind of friend I needed
*   for a while.*
When it spoke too strongly
*   I would close it*
*   put it back upon the shelf*
*   take it down another day*
*   when I was ready.*

But one day my friend who'd led me to the book
*   stabbed me to life*
*   to join him in getting on with the journey*
*   of becoming who we are.*
He was the pathleader I didn't know I needed.

Loving

Can friends be in love
in special ways?
There is such a thin line
between liking
and loving.
The difference
I suppose
is that friends can love each other
without being lovers.

BEGINNINGS

*There is no one way
for friendships to start
but they have to start some way.*

Beginnings

We were there
        admiring the same picture in the gallery.
She smiled
        and I said something about liking Cézanne.
                 o   o   o

After the meeting
        he said he liked my stand on spending.
I explained why
        turns out we both grew up in the depression.
                 o   o   o

We sat together
        at the United Way fund-raising party.
It so happens
        neither of us liked fund-raising
                or parties, for that matter.
                 o   o   o

We cheered together winters
        watching our kids play hockey.
The same in summers
        at Little League diamonds.
                 o   o   o

We marched together
        for peace
lobbied Congress for the nuclear freeze
        and a ban on testing.
                 o   o   o

There is no one way
        for friendships to start
but they have to start some way.

Chance Encounter

They met at the airline check-in counter
when the plane was late
and she needed help with her bags.
She was from another land
and he was old enough to be her father
but they had the courage to talk
and to share a little of their lives.
They parted
friends.

Chance Not Taken

We pass each other
    in the aisle of a store
    in the waiting room
        of the doctor's office
    in the hall between our offices.

Sometimes our eyes meet
    perhaps we smile
    and say a word or two
        but nothing more.

What unnamed fears constrain our hearts
    from knowing someone new?
What risks seem much too great to take
    in making friends?

Testing

She left her seclusion of loneliness
            and moved into friendship
like a yearling doe
        moving from the dark forest
        into the clearing.
Tentative at first
        unsure
listening for the unknowns
        testing the quiet
        watching for danger signs
needing the warmth that was there
        but poised to run away
                if there was harm.

Friendship's Fair Exchange

They were five-year-olds that first day in school.
He had a birthmark on his face;
    she wore thick glasses for weak eyes.
She asked what the red blotch was;
    he said it proved he was born.
He asked why she wore such funny glasses;
    she said so that she could see.
Having settled all that
    they became friends.

Not A Matter Of Age

We didn't even know each other
                yet.
But there we were
                laughing uncontrollably
when everyone else had stopped.
Who was this
                bubbling over
Her laugh spoke volumes
                sparked such life in me.
I was old enough to be her mother—
                Could we be friends?

In a few weeks
her age was like her
                blond hair
                brown eyes
                    and
                Swedishness.
Just another fact.

How could age matter — we had so much else.

Conflicts Within

Such reaching out
*   such holding back*
so many doubts
*   so many things to know*
so much to share
*   so much to hide*
such openness and secrecy combined.
Such a desperate need for friends
*   yet wanting to be only yourself.*

It's like that
*   at thirteen.*

Respecting

I can respect you
*   and never seek you as a friend*
but I can never seek you as a friend
*   unless I respect you.*

NURTURING

*Understanding friends are magic mirrors
to help us see ourselves.*

How It Is With Us

*I seek her out
when I have doubts about my life
wanting to be listened to
      and reassured
needing confidence restored.*

*She seeks me out
when she feels sobered by the world
and wants to laugh again
at silly things we talk about.*

*I seek her out
to brag about some small success I've had
knowing she'll not think me vain
      but understand.*

*She seeks me out
to help her ponder choices in her life
to talk outloud
to test the consequences of an act.*

*That's how it is with us
      each special to the other.*

On Call

By actual count
we see each other thirteen times a year
> *the final Friday night of every month*
> *when we join others in our poker club*
and on December twenty-first
> *the night we set aside*
> *to treat our wives with dinner out.*
But more than any other in the club
he is a special friend
for reasons I don't really understand.
We jab each other with our bets
> *some based on hands we hold*
> *and some on bluff*
and make derisive commentaries
about the other's playing skill.
And though we never seek the other's company
> *the weeks between*
we somehow know that each of us
will be on call
to help the other out
> *if there is need.*
That's the kind of friends we are.

Confession

Weary of hours of producing
        blank pages,
I'd cross the street to my friend's who'd set before me
        baked creations
                whipped up in minutes.

We'd talk a mile a minute
she intent on her thoughts
I on mine
we often talked past each other.
Like sisters
        we argued
                not sure what about
        we apologized
                not sure what for.
Something was not right.

Then one day I blurted out I wanted to be
        like her.
She shot back she wanted to be
        like me.

We understood each other after that.

Unspoken Words

I think it is the way she listens
                    totally
with head slightly turned
and eyes reflecting each emotion
                    with complete fidelity
and with no warning signs
to turn me off before I'm through.
Perhaps it is the way she senses moods
without insisting on an explanation
but accepting one if given.
Or is it the way she confides in me
letting me in on the wavelengths of her life
to better understand the whole of her.

We met by casual accident
                    some years ago
two strangers in a crowd when introduced
and not remembering now the words we spoke.
Perhaps unspoken words revealed our needs
and let the other know
that there were gifts of caring
wrapped and stored inside our souls
                    waiting to be given.

A Feast

I have a hunger
to hear laughter at foolish things
> *to see tears of honest compassion*
>> *to feel the warmth of nearness.*

I have a hunger
to share thoughts
> *compare notes*
>> *dream dreams.*

When I am with you
I feast on your friendship.

Husband And Wife

He's in
> *Who's Who In America.*
I still struggle with
> *Who I Am.*
He's a doer.
> *Does that make me a thinker?*

Opposites attract, they say.
Yet I never dreamed we'd have to work
> *at being friends.*

Friendship Pledge

We promised
when we were young
        more innocent than wise
that we'd be friends for life.
We said we'd keep in touch
no matter where we were.
We said there'd be no secrets in our hearts
we couldn't share.
We said all that and more
                when we were young
and signed our friendship pledge in blood
flowing from a pinprick in our thumbs.
Now
having reached the autumn of our years
that pledge is still as bright
                as then.

Accepting

You withhold harsh judgment of me
when I am late for our meeting
or break away from my diet
or don't wear a hat in the rain.

You do not denounce me
when I forget your birthday
or put too much salt on my eggs
or make the wrong turn off 37th street.

You accept the total package that is me
my virtues and faults
my strengths and weaknesses
my generosity and selfishness.

*Is that **why** we are friends*
*or **because** we are friends?*

Giving-Receiving

The Scriptures say
it is more blessed to give
          than to receive,
but how can that be true with friends.
Giving and receiving are as one
          a single caring act
not possible
unless the giver is also
willing to receive.

Honoring

Strangers have honored me
for small achievements in my life.
You have honored me
by urging me to risk higher goals
knowing I might fail.

Understanding

When she understood his drive to win
he found ways to help others succeed.

When he understood her fear of failure
she found courage to be herself.

When she understood his need for love
he became a more loving man.

When he understood her moments of doubt
she became a more confident woman.

Understanding friends are magic mirrors
to help us see ourselves.

Appreciating

Appreciation
> *lifts spirits*
> *rekindles faith*
> *costs nothing*
> *can be given often*
> *and is one habit worth having.*
Friends practice it.

Touching

You tell me that you care
you understand
you want to be my friend.

You tell me this
          and more
without a word
when you touch my hand.

Holding

We are all children
        wanting to be held
and there are times
you hold me close
        and comfort me with friendship
though we are miles apart.

Sharing

Through all the years
they shared the debits and credits of their friendship
without ever figuring the balance
    at the end of the day.

Wondering

Tell me. . .
Does our Creator provide friends
>*not only to share the journey*
>*but to give us a taste*
>>*of what will be*
>>*when we are fully known?*

Cheering

You are there
along the sidelines of my life
cheering me on
         no matter what the race.

You are there
in the grandstand of my world
and I hear your voice
         even in the crowd.

You are there
inside my soul
cheering softly
              softly
                       softly
and I hear.

ENDINGS

A friendship, like life itself,
has a beginning,
a time of growth and nurturing,
and an ending,
though there may be pain and sadness
the ending has come about.

Changing Wants

She wanted his strength and his wisdom
> *so much like her father.*
As she grew stronger and wiser
she tested her wings
> *and flew away.*
It was harder to be friends
> *after that.*

Betrayal

He gave her secrets of his heart
        for keeping safe
but late one night
she shared them with another
        and they came back to him.

They still are friends
        of sorts
but he will never again share
        his secrets.

Wanting More

They had been friends so long
so sure of how it was
*   with the other.*

And then one day
*   without a word*
he walked away.

She said
I think he wanted more from me
*   than friendship*
and that was more than I could give.

The Same But Different

He lived in a house
        on a hill.
His friend lived
        on the other side of town.
His family took Florida vacations.
His friend's went fishing on the river.

These things didn't bother them
        when they were growing up in school,
but something changed after that.
Everything was the same
        but different.

Displacement

You had room in your life
for three close friends
including me.
Then someone came along
offering something new
and I became a former friend,
a victim of life's law of displacement.

A Time To Say Good-Bye

We came together
searching for meaning in our lives
 two of us among the many
challenging faiths
wondering about life and death
 and life after death.

My search has ended now.
I've found the answers that I sought.
Your search goes on
but you still challenge answers I have found.
Instead of friends
 who searched for meaning in it all
we have become opponents in debate.
We'd better say good-bye.

Beyond Repair

Finally
when I spoke my mind
and he spoke his
we saw each other
at last.
We broke apart
cleanly
two separate pieces.

We began to accept
just barely
who the other was.
Caring glued us back together
fragilely.

The next time it happened
we shattered
into a thousand pieces.
There was nothing left to mend.

The Gap Of Time

There was such wild excitement
        such sweet anticipation
knowing we would meet again
                close friends
ignoring all those years
when fate had intervened
to keep us apart.

Surely in a little while
we'd bridge the gap of time
        sharing dreams
        making plans.

Surely in a little while
we'd be the way we were
                wouldn't we?
                        wouldn't we?

POSTSCRIPT

To Hadley, My Co-Author: New Beginnings

Remember our talk
when I felt empty and alone
myself hidden from myself
yet longing to be understood
and you urged me to create,
to write poems about friendship.

Remember my reply
that by the time I write poetry
you won't be here
and you said
you would be.

You are here
inside my soul
cheering me on
and I hear.

Mary Klaaren Andersen

Greater love has no man than this,
that a man lay down his life for his friends.

No longer do I call you servants
for the servant does not know what his master is doing;
but I have called you friends,
for all that I have heard from my Father
I have made known to you.

The Gospel According to John
Chapter 15, verses 13 & 15